Wordwise and Wordwise+

Word Processing Handbooks

Wordwise and Wordwise+

Wendy Chuter

Pitman

Computer Handbooks

The complete list of titles in this series and the Pitman
Pocket Guide series appears after the Index at the
end of this Handbook. The Publishers would
welcome suggestions for further additions and
improvements to the series.

PITMAN PUBLISHING LIMITED
128 Long Acre, London WC2E 9AN

Associated Companies
Pitman Publishing Pty Ltd, Melbourne
Pitman Publishing New Zealand Ltd, Wellington
Copp Clark Pitman, Toronto

First edition 1985

British Library Cataloguing in Publication Data

Chuter, Wendy
    Wordwise and Wordwise+. — (Computer handbooks)
    1. Microcomputer   2. Word processing
    I. Title   II. Series
    652'.5'0285404   Z52.5.B35

    ISBN 0 273 02300 4

Printed in Great Britain at the Bath Press, Avon

Contents

How to Use This Handbook

This Handbook is intended to provide a quick-reference facility for those possessing a BBC microcomputer model B (32K) with a WORDWISE or WORDWISE PLUS ROM fitted. The ROM is a chip which contains all the necessary functions to operate as a word processor and does not take up any space in the working memory of the computer.

Existing Wordwise users can get their present chip upgraded by returning the original ROM and manual to Computer Concepts, Gaddesden Place, Hemel Hempstead, Herts, HP2 6EX. The cost of this upgrade is £24.15 at the time of writing. The Wordwise Plus chip has some new embedded commands such as Fully Indent, Underline, Double strike print, numbering the lines on the screen in Preview Mode, Pause and Print File. There is also the facility to split the working memory into segments; up to 10 segments can be used containing text or programs. Also included with the new package are some programs which enable you to mail merge, create an index, print out in two columns and use continuous processing. The saving and loading of text has been speeded up and a warning before a document is overwritten, in memory or on disk, has been added.

Technical terms are explained with examples, and the use of jargon is avoided where possible. Both the beginner and the experienced user should find this Handbook easy to follow.

The facilities of WORDWISE have been grouped under the following headings:

Preliminaries: getting started, status line, cursor controls
Creating: insert, overwrite, correcting errors, embedded commands, user-defined keys
Editing: setting markers, case change, global or selective replacement, previewing
Storage and Retrieval: disk usage, saving, loading, spooling, printers and printing
Segments: usage of the segments

Key to Instructions Used in this Handbook

☐	indicates what should appear on the screen. On occasions, only the main headings will be shown
__ (underscore)	shows the position of the cursor on the screen
BOLD PRINT	indicates keys to be pressed by the operator
<CTRL>	means that the CONTROL key must be held down while another key is pressed
<SHIFT>	means that the SHIFT key must be held down while another key is pressed
< >	indicates use of a key

f0	indicates the use of that red function key
+	only applies if WORDWISE PLUS is fitted

Note: It is important when following the examples contained in this Handbook to position the cursor in exactly the place shown. The action to be taken, after the placement of the cursor, is shown sequentially after the screen box. An example is shown below:

To insert a character

Te cursor is a flashing	(text on the screen)

position your cursor as shown above (that is, underneath the letter 'e').

h (this means type the letter 'h')

Preliminaries

Switch on the computer. If the WORDWISE ROM has been correctly fitted, your screen should indicate that you are working in the BASIC language.

```
BBC Computer 32K
Acorn DFS
BASIC
>_
```

If the top line of the display is off the screen, type the following:

*TV 255 <RETURN>

Call up WORDWISE:

*WORDWISE <RETURN> (or *W.) <RETURN>

will suffice.

Old text? (Y/N) appears in WORDWISE only. Answer no as you have yet to key in any text.

N (only applicable to WORDWISE)

The main menu is now displayed showing you the options available. To select an option you type the relevant number; that option will begin to flash to confirm your selection. If you use the wrong key, then press <ESCAPE> (located on the top left side of the keyboard) to cancel your choice.

WORDWISE
1) Save entire text
2) Load new text
3) Save marked text
4) Load text to cursor
5) Search and Replace
6) Print text
7) Preview text
8) Spool text

ESC Edit Mode

Please enter choice_

+

```
WORDWISE PLUS
1) Save entire text
2) Load new text
3) Save marked text
4) Load text to cursor
5) Search and Replace
6) Print text
7) Preview text
8) Spool text
9) Segment menu

ESC Edit Mode

Please enter choice_
```

To start entering text, select Edit Mode

<ESCAPE>

```
Words   Characters free 24562 I

Start
-
End
```

+

```
Words 0 Characters free 24068 I

Start
-
End
```

5

BREAK key

If at any time during your word processing you wish to resume using the computer in its BASIC state, press <CTRL> and <BREAK> together, or type *BASIC (*B. will suffice). If you use this it may mean the loss of your text in the current memory.

ESCAPE key

When the main menu is displayed upon the screen, pressing <ESCAPE> will take you into Edit Mode and vice versa; this is known as a toggle action. The ESCAPE key can also be used to cancel an option from the menu or to discontinue printing or previewing.

Auto-repeat keys

As with electric/electronic typewriters, the BBC microcomputer keys are auto-repeat. This means that if you keep your finger on a key it will continuously repeat that particular key.

Mode 7

Edit Mode uses the BBC microcomputer's Mode 7 facility which provides 40 characters across the screen. This is not how the final document will appear. You may, therefore, get a ragged left-hand margin at this stage. Do not try to correct this as later it will be done automatically.

Wordwrap

WORDWISE has a wordwrap facility which means you must not use the RETURN key at the end of a screen line; only use it when you require a new paragraph or a blank line. Furthermore, WORDWISE will ensure that only complete words appear at the end of each line. If, when making corrections, the line endings do not wrap properly, then moving the cursor up or down will correct this.

Status line

The top line of the screen shows you the status line. As you key in text, the number of words will appear indicating how many you have typed in your document. This can be of help if you have to write a report of 500 words. The characters free denotes the number of character spaces still available in the computer's memory. The letter 'I' denotes that you are in Insert Mode which WORDWISE will always default to when you first switch on. To the right of the letter 'I' will appear any markers that you use during your editing of the document. The status line is also used by the computer to ask you questions, for example, 'Are you sure?' you wish to delete marked text.

Start and End

This shows you how your document stands at the moment. Any text you enter will be placed between these two words. The small flashing line on the screen is called the cursor and this shows you where the printing point is on the screen. When editing your document the cursor needs to be moved as quickly as possible, and the necessary cursor movements are shown on page 9.

Screen display

As previously mentioned, your text is displayed on the screen with a width of 40 characters. As you key in, your text will move up the screen to enable more to be displayed. Eventually, some of it will disappear off the top of the screen. Don't worry, you haven't lost this, it is still in the computer's memory. The screen can only display 23 lines of text at a time — referred to as a screenful. Moving the cursor up or down will enable you to view different parts of your document.

Cursor control

The cursor is moved about the document by using the arrowed keys on the keyboard. After creating text (*see* page 10) the following cursor controls can be carried out. You should try and find the quickest way of moving the cursor to the required position.

Cursor to?

The red function key *f4* can be used to move the
cursor quickly to a specified character. The
computer will only search from the current cursor
position forwards. When *f4* is pressed, the question
'Move Cursor to?' will appear in the status line.
Pressing a letter key, *f1*, *f2*, punctuation mark or even
the RETURN key will move the cursor forward to the
next occurrence of this character. This facility can be
used if you wish to move to the end of a paragraph
quickly. Pressing *f4* followed by the RETURN key will
do this for you.

Following is a summary of these quick cursor
controls.

→	will move the cursor one character to the right
←	will move the cursor one character to the left
↑	will move the cursor one line up
↓	will move the cursor one line down
<CTRL> and →	will move the cursor one word to the right
<CTRL> and ←	will move the cursor one word to the left
<CTRL> and ↑	will move the cursor up one screenful (23 lines)
<CTRL> and ↓	will move the cursor down one screenful
<SHIFT> and →	will move the cursor to the right end of line

<SHIFT> and ←	will move the cursor to the left end of line
<SHIFT> and ↑	will move the cursor to start of the text
<SHIFT> and ↓	will move the cursor to end of the text
f4 and (a character, e.g. <RETURN>, *f1*, *f2*, full stop)	will move the cursor to the next occurrence of that character

Creating Text

```
Words    Characters free 24562 I

Start
-
End
```

+

```
Words 0 Characters free 24068 I

Start
-
End
```

From this position (*see* page 5), you can simply type in text. Note that the BBC Micro, when first switched on, will produce capital letters unless you depress CAPS LOCK before typing. The red light beneath the letters 'caps lock' on the keyboard will go out.

Inserting

You can insert character(s), word(s), paragraph(s) or previously saved text into your current document. If you have WORDWISE PLUS fitted, you can also insert text from a segment into the main text area or from one segment to another. Check that the letter I appears in the status line at the top of the screen (press *f0* once if O appears in the status line).

The screen boxes below contain example text to demonstrate insertion. Ensure that you position the cursor one character to the right of where you wish the insertion to take place as shown in the examples.

To insert character(s)

| Te cursor is a flashing |

h

To insert word(s)

| The cursor is a flashing |

small<SPACE BAR>

The space bar was tapped once to insert a space after the inserted word.

To insert paragraph(s)

The cursor is a small flashing line that
   indicates the next typing position.

It is very important that you learn how
to move the cursor quickly about the
document to make editing easier.

Key in the missing paragraph and <RETURN> twice
to obtain a new paragraph and a blank line
between.

The cursor is a small flashing line that
   indicates the next typing position.

By using the arrowed keys in conjunction
   with either the control or shift key it
   is possible to move the cursor about
quickly.

It is very important that you learn how
to move the cursor quickly about the
document to make editing easier.

To insert previously saved text
Position your cursor at the point in your current
document where you wish a previously saved
document to be inserted. Make sure the disk or tape
containing this previously saved document is in the
disk drive or cassette player. <ESCAPE> to the Main
Menu and select option 4. 'Please enter filename'
appears on the screen. Answer the question with the
name of the previously saved document.

Name of your previously saved document
<RETURN>

(If using a tape system, press PLAY on the recorder.)

<ESCAPE> to Edit Mode

To insert text from a segment **+ only** (*see* segments, page 80)
It is possible to create text in one of the segments and then insert it into your main text or another segment.

Edit Mode

Position the cursor where you wish the segment to be inserted.

<ESCAPE> to main menu

Type **:TYPE SEGMENT n** <RETURN> where n is the segment number containing the text to be inserted.

    Press any key as instructed.

    <ESCAPE> to Edit Mode and check that the insertion has taken place.

    Note: Any embedded commands in the inserted text may affect any subsequent main text.

Deleting

WORDWISE has the facility to delete either character(s), word(s) or a marked section of text. WORDWISE PLUS has the extra facilities of deleting a sentence or a paragraph without the need for setting markers. When the deletion takes place, the resulting space is closed up. There are two ways of deleting characters and words. When using the black DELETE key, the cursor needs to be one character to the right of the incorrect character. The cursor remains stationary so that you can carry on deleting the character to the left of the cursor. Be careful when deleting by this method because the DELETE key is an Auto-Repeat key and you can delete more than you require.

The second method involves the use of the CTRL key and one other key. To correct a single letter, place the cursor beneath the incorrect character. The cursor remains stationary so that you can carry on deleting the character above the cursor.

To delete character(s)

Thre cursor is a flashing

<DELETE>

or

Thre cursor is a flashing

<CTRL>**A**

TRY 27 82 83 (12)

2x P 50 1

27 30 (12)

ESC 30 (12)

ESC & IE & C

& IB   "   "

Printer driver location & 222

To delete word(s)

> The cursor is a small s̲mall flashing

<CTRL>**D**

The cursor can be underneath any character of the word to be deleted. If you require several words to be deleted, you may find it quicker to use the next method.

To delete a sentence

> Wordwise Plus is a ROM chip manufactured by Computer Concepts.̲ It has many advantages over the previous Wordwise chip. It has the extra facilities such as further embedded commands to turn on and off underlining.

Position the cursor as shown.

f6 In the status line appears 'Delete to?'
. (type a full stop)
<CTRL> **A** to delete the full stop

To delete a paragraph

The cursor is a small flashing line that
   indicates the next typing position.

_

By using the arrowed keys in conjunction
   with either the control or shift key
it is possible to move the cursor about
quickly.

It is very important that you learn how
to move the cursor quickly about the
document to make editing easier.

Position your cursor as shown.

f6
<RETURN>
↓ (Move the cursor down one line)
<DELETE><DELETE> to remove the line spaces

To delete a marked section
It is possible to delete a marked section of text by
setting markers at the start and end of that text. If the
marked section is more than 250 characters long,
including the spaces and returns, then the question
'Are you sure?' will appear on the status line. By
answering Y to this question the marked section will
be deleted. This is a safeguard to stop you
accidentally deleting more than you require. When
you have set the two markers, they will appear on the
status line. If you try deleting without setting the
markers, then a question will appear on the status

line asking where they are. The markers will be
deleted at the same time as the deleted section.
Below is an example of a marked section to be
deleted.

The cursor is a small flashing line that
   indicates the next typing position. ■ By
   using the arrowed keys in conjunction
with either the control or shift key it
is possible to move the cursor about
quickly.■ !t is very important that you
learn how to move the cursor quickly
about the document to make editing
easier.

Move the cursor to the start of the text you wish to
delete.

f3 will set the marker

Move the cursor to the end of text you wish to delete.

f3 will set the marker
f7 will delete the marked section

Overwriting

This facility enables you to overwrite the original text at the position of the cursor. When you first enter WORDWISE the insert mode is automatically turned on. If you look at the status line you will notice that an 'I' (insert) appears. By pressing *f0* you can change to overwrite mode; an 'O' (overwrite) will appear on the status line. When overwrite mode is not required it is best to return to insert mode to avoid accidental overtyping of text you wish to retain.

> The cussor is a small flashing

f0 notice in the status line the letter 'O' has appeared in place of 'I'
r
f0 (if you have finished with overwrite mode)

Embedded Commands

When you start keying in text, WORDWISE is in Edit Mode, which means that there are 40 characters across the screen. However, this is not how your document will appear in the final printed version.

The embedded commands are instructions to the printer specifying how you wish your finished document to look (e.g. line length, page length, indentation etc.) and can be entered at any time in your text while in Edit Mode. These commands will not be shown in the final print out; they will not take effect while you are in Edit Mode. However, when you are previewing text (*see* page 67) the embedded commands will be interpreted showing how your work will appear in print.

If you are using a colour monitor, the embedded commands will appear as green characters on the screen. If using a monochrome monitor, they will appear as grey.

You must remember that when printing takes place, the embedded commands are only acted upon as the document is printed out. Therefore if you enter the embedded command for the line length at the bottom of the document it would have no effect upon the print out; it would default to its standard value (*see* later notes on embedded commands). Similarly, if you wanted to change the line length in the middle of a document, by inserting an embedded command at the chosen point, it would change from that point onwards.

To enter the embedded commands you must first press *f1* (green embedded command start), enter the required command and then press *f2* (white embedded command end). More than one command can be entered at a time. In this instance, instead of pressing *f2* at the end of each command, press *f1* between each different command and then *f2* when you have finished. Here is an example for entering more than one embedded command:

*f1*LL50*f1*PL50*f1*LM10*f2*

If a number needs to be entered, you should not leave a space between it and the letters. You must avoid keying in the embedded commands in such a way that they run onto two lines. If you make a mistake while entering the embedded commands you can correct it in exactly the same way as you would for correcting text.

The commands can be entered in either upper or lower case. If your text does not return to its normal colour after entering an embedded command it may be because you have forgotten to press *f2* to end the embedded command. Likewise, if when deleting text near an embedded command it changes colour, it may be because you have deleted the keystroke *f2*. By pressing *f2* at the end of the embedded command it should return the text to its normal colour.

The following pages list the embedded commands, their default values and examples of the way the text will look before and after they have been entered.

The default value is that value assumed by the computer if particular embedded commands are omitted. For example, if a line length command is not included in your document, a length of 70 characters is assumed. There is a summary of these embedded commands on page 93.

Begin Page

Entered as BP.

This embedded command instructs the printer to start a new page at any given point in your document. It forces a new page to begin in a chosen position, such as a continuation sheet or a new chapter. This will only work if the embedded command to enable paging has also been used. The command should be placed at the point you wish to start a new page. If you enter the command followed by a RETURN it will give you an extra blank line at the top of the next page. If you wish your last page of a document to be numbered or the footer to be printed, it is necessary to insert *f1*BP (no *f2* or RETURN) at the end of the text. Otherwise the printer will finish in the middle of a page.

Bottom Space

Entered as BSn where n is a value of the number of lines required in the bottom space.

Defaults to 6.

This embedded command sets the space which you require to be left blank at the bottom of each page (if using single sheets). It will only function if you use the Enable Paging command. This command must be considered with those of page length and top space. If you have a page length of 58, top space of 6 and bottom space of 6, then there will only be 46 lines of text on each page. The top and bottom spaces are added together and deducted from the page length (*see* the illustration below).

$$
\left.
\begin{array}{l}
1\\
2\\
3\\
4\\
5\\
6
\end{array}
\right\} \text{Top Space}
$$

Text 46 lines

Page Length 58 Lines

$$
\left.
\begin{array}{l}
1\\
2\\
3\\
4\\
5\\
6
\end{array}
\right\} \text{Bottom Space}
$$

If you use the Define Footer, it will be printed out in the Bottom Space in the Footing Position.

Cancel all Indents

Entered as CI.

   This embedded command will cancel any indent command which has previously been entered.

Edit Mode

This section of text was indented ten
spaces by a previously entered embedded
command. *f1CIf2*

The cancel all indents embedded command
causes following text to be blocked at
the left-hand margin.

Preview Mode

               This section of text was indented ten
               spaces by a previously entered embedded
               command.

The cancel all indents embedded command causes
following text to be blocked at the left-hand
margin.

Centre

Entered as CE for a single centred line or CEn where n is the number of lines to be centred.

Defaults to 1.

This embedded command will centre text horizontally on the current line length. This facility is useful for centring titles, subject headings, etc.

Edit Mode

> *f1*CE*f2*WORDWISE

Preview Mode

> WORDWISE

If you use CEn then you must use <RETURN> at the end of each line to be centred. For example:

Edit Mode

> *f1*CE2*f2*Wordwise<RETURN>
> Word Processing Chip<RETURN>

Preview Mode

> Wordwise
> Word Processing Chip

You may wish to have your headers and footers centred; before they can be centred you must first define them (*see* Define Footer on page 26 and Define Header on page 28). For example:

*f1*DH*f1*CE*f2*   or   *f1*DF*f1*CE*f2*

Centring an underlined piece of text can sometimes cause problems by making the underscore go from the left margin instead of just under the centred text.

Edit Mode

> *f1*CE*f1*OCn*f2*Wordwise*f1*OCn*f2* (where OCn is your

printer command to underline)

or if WORDWISE PLUS

Edit Mode

> *f1*CE*f1*US*f2*Wordwise*f1*UE*f2*

In Preview Mode this will show

> Wordwise

By using a pad character command (*see* page 42) between the commands you will overcome this problem. For example:

*f1*CE*f2*||*f1*OCn*f2*Wordwise or
(**+**) *f1*CE*f2*||*f1*US*f2*Wordwise

will appear in Preview Mode as

> <u>Wordwise</u>

Conditional Page

Entered as CP and a number.

This embedded command will ensure that a new page is started even if there are a number of lines still remaining. It can be used to make sure that particular parts of text are not split up onto two pages, e.g. a table of figures. The number entered is the number of lines in the text that you do not wish to be split. This command must be used with the embedded command to enable paging and it will take into account your Page Length and Bottom Space embedded commands.

For example, *f1*CP15*f2* will ensure that the next 15 lines of text (i.e. 15 lines of text in Preview Mode) will not be split between two pages.

Continuous Output

Entered as CO.

Defaults to ON.

This embedded command will enable you to use continuous paper when printing out. However, any headings, footings, page length, page numbers, etc. will be omitted.

Define Footer

Entered as DF.

Defaults to the third line of the bottom space if Footing Position is not entered.

WORDWISE PLUS defaults to printing and centring 'Page n', where n is the number of the page.

This embedded command will ensure that any text entered after this command up to the first <RETURN> will be printed at the foot of every page. It is printed in the Bottom Space. For example:

*f1*DF*f2* 1st January 1985 <RETURN>

This command will ensure that this date is printed in the Footing Position of every page.

If you are using WORDWISE the command can be used in conjunction with the Page Number and Print Page commands. For example:

*f1*DF*f1*PN*f1*PP*f2*<RETURN>

This command will ensure that the page number is printed at the foot of every page. The number will be printed at the left margin and will be incremented automatically.

If you prefer your page number to be centred, then enter

*f1*DF*f1*CE*f1*PN*f1*PP*f2*<RETURN>

When using WORDWISE PLUS you may prefer to omit the word 'Page' before the number. To do this, enter

*f1*DF*f1*PP*f2*<RETURN>

to print the page number at the left margin, or

*f1*DF*f1*CE*f1*PP*f2*<RETURN>

to centre the page number.

When using the Define Footer command, to enable the last footer to be printed out you must enter *f1*BP (without *f2* or <RETURN>) at the end of the text. This will prevent the printer from finishing in the middle of a page.

Define Header

Entered as DH.

Defaults to the third line of the top space if Heading Position is not entered.

This embedded command will ensure that any text entered after this command up to the first <RETURN> will be printed at the head of every page. It is printed in the Top Space. For example:

*f1*DH*f2* 1st January 1985<RETURN>

will ensure that the date is printed in the Heading Position on every page.

It can be used in conjunction with the page numbering and centring commands if you wish to centre your page number at the head of your page. For example:

Edit Mode
*f1*DH*f1*CE*f1*PP*f2*<RETURN>

Define Pound sign

Entered as DPn where n is the value of the code necessary for the printer to print a pound sign.

Defaults to 96.

This embedded command is used to ensure that any pound signs in your text are printed. It is necessary to enter the embedded command before every pound sign in your document. By referring to your printer manual, you will be able to find which ASCII code is required for your printer to print the pound sign. (The ASCII codes are dealt with in more detail on page 77.) For example, the Epson uses the code 35 so the embedded command is entered as *f1*DP35*f2*. However, some printers will print a pound sign simply by keying-in a # (hash) in place of the pound sign in your text. Alternatively, if your printer contains dip-switches, then these can be adjusted to the UK character set.

Define Tab stops

Entered as DTn (or DTn,n if you require more than one tab setting) where n is the value of your tab setting.

Defaults to 10,20,30, and in 10s thereafter.

This embedded command allows you to set up to nine tab settings (fourteen in WORDWISE PLUS) and will help you with any display or column work. As the default value is set in 10s you are really re-defining those already set. If you wish to enter more than one tab setting, then separate them with commas. You can change your previously set tab settings simply by typing in the embedded command again but with different settings. The TAB key on the computer keyboard is used to move from one tab setting to the next, and while in Edit Mode this will appear as an arrow on the screen. If you wish to tab past a setting, then press the tab key twice. For example:

Edit Mode

```
f1DT21,31,42f2→a→a→a<RETURN>
→a→a→a
```

Preview Mode

a	a	a
a	a	a

Disable Message

Entered as DM.

   Defaults to ON.

   This embedded command will stop the 'Paper!' message appearing on the screen during the Preview Mode and print out. It is the opposite of EM. *See* EM command on page 32.

Double-strike End +

Entered as DE.

   Defaults to Epson printer and related printers.
Control codes sent are 27,72 or <ESC> H.

   This embedded command is used to instruct the
printer to turn off the double strike. You must
remember to use the DE command at the end of the
required double-strike text to turn it off, otherwise
the rest of your document will be printed in double-
strike mode. *See* DS command.

   WORDWISE users can obtain Double strike End by
entering OC27,72 if using an Epson printer. *See*
Output Control code on page 42.

Double-strike Start +

Entered as DS.

   Defaults to Epson printer and related printers.
Control codes sent are 27,71 or <ESC> G.

   This embedded command is used to turn on the
double-strike if your printer has this facility. During
the printing out, the text entered after this command
will be overtyped to give a darker effect. In your
printer manual it might also be called emphasized or
bold print. When previewing text the double-strike
text will be shown as negative on the screen, i.e.
white background with black letters. This embedded
command has been set to work with Epson or Epson-
compatible printers.

   WORDWISE users can obtain Double strike Start
by entering OC27,71 if using an Epson printer. *See*
Output Control code on page 42.

Enable Message

Entered as EM.

   Defaults to NO message.

   This embedded command is used to display a
message ('Paper!') on the screen and to make the
computer beep to tell you to insert another single
sheet of paper. This is only used when you are
printing out using single sheets rather than
continuous stationery. It is the opposite of DM. It must
be entered at the beginning of a document along
with EP. When previewing text, if EM command is not
used the text will quickly scroll through the
document. If only EM and not EP is used, then the
message will only appear at the end of the text.

Enable Paging

Entered as EP.

   Defaults to OFF.

   This embedded command is used to instruct the
computer and printer that you wish your document to
be split into single sheets of paper or paged blocks
on continuous stationery. This command must be
entered at the top of your text, especially if you wish
to enter the command for defining a header. When
previewing text you will be able to see where one
page finishes and the next begins and change this if
required using the BP command.

Footing Position

Entered as FPn where n is a value between 0 and the Bottom Space value.

Defaults to the third line of the bottom space.

This embedded command is used when you wish the Defined Footer to be printed in a different place to that of the default value. It will only work if you have first used the commands EP and DF. If your FP value is larger than the BS value, then the footer will not be printed. For example:

Edit Mode
*f1*PL50*f1*EM*f1*EP*f1*DF*f1*CE*f2* 1st January
1985<RETURN>

will result in the following page being displayed in Preview Mode.

	1
	2
Top space	3
	4
	5
	6
Text 38 lines	
	1
	2
Bottom space	1st January 1985
	4
	5
	6

Changing the footing position by entering *f1FP6f2* to the line of embedded commands will result in the following in Preview Mode:

	1
	2
Top space	3
	4
	5
	6
Text 38 lines	
	1
	2
Bottom space	3
	4
	5
	1st January 1985

Fully Indent +

Entered as FI.

This embedded command is used when you wish to align your text to the right margin. All the text entered to the <RETURN> will be printed this way. For example:

Edit Mode

```
f1FIf2 1 High Street<RETURN>
f1FIf2 Newtown <RETURN>
f1FIf2 Hants<RETURN>
```

```
                                        1 High Street
                                            Newtown
                                              Hants
```

Notice how the right margin is now straight.

Get File

Entered as GF"name of the document".

This embedded command can be used in a document to instruct the computer at print-out time to find a particular file on disk or tape, and print it in the selected position in your document. Remember to use the quotation marks as you would when loading a BASIC program. The command is acted upon during Preview Mode, so if you are using disk you must have the appropriate one containing that file in the drive (or tape in the data recorder).

The Get File command can be used to call up standard paragraphs stored on disk or tape, and inserted into your document where required. For example, your address could be stored as a standard paragraph and called up each time you type a letter.

This command can also be used for defining footers and headers that are more than one line of text in length. You will have to enter the command on every page.

35

However, if you have any other embedded commands in the file that you get, the commands will not be acted upon and will be printed out instead. If you wish the embedded commands to be acted upon, then use the Print File embedded command instead.

Heading Position

Entered as HPn where n is a value between 0 and the Top Space value.

Defaults to the third line of the top space.

This embedded command is used when you wish the defined header to be printed in a different place to the default value. It will only work if you have first used the commands EP and DH. If your HP value is larger than the TS value, the header will not be printed. For example:

Edit Mode
*f1*PL50*f1*EM*f1*EP*f1*DH*f1*CE*f2* 1st January 1985<RETURN>

will result in the following being displayed in Preview Mode:

```
                              1
                              2
Top space             1st January 1985
                              4
                              5
                              6

Text 38 lines
                              1
                              2
Bottom space                  3
                              4
                              5
                              6
```

Changing the heading position by entering *f1*HP6*f2* to the line of embedded commands will result in the following in Preview Mode:

```
                              1
                              2
Top space                     3
                              4
                              5
                      1st January 1985
Text 38 lines
                              1
                              2
Bottom space                  3
                              4
                              5
                              6
```

Indent

Entered as INn where n is the number of character spaces to be indented from the left margin.

This embedded command is used when you wish to insert text instead of changing the left margin. The text will remain in this new position until the command to cancel indent (CI) is used. If the command is entered in mid-line, the indentation will start on the next line. If only the first line of text is required to be indented it is better to use the command for a temporary indent. For example:

Edit Mode

> *f1*LM10*f2* This text will be blocked at the left margin which has been set at 10.<RETURN>
>
> *f1*IN10*f2* This text will appear ten spaces from the left margin which then gives a left margin of 20.

Preview Mode

> This text will be blocked at the left margin which has been set at 10.
>
>   This text will appear ten
>   spaces from the left margin
>   which then gives a left margin
>   of 20.

38

Justify On

Entered as JO.

Defaults to ON.

This embedded command will produce a straight right margin, similar to the left margin. The computer works out how many extra spaces are required to make the right margin end in the same place each time, and distributes them evenly along the line. When reading justified text you will notice the extra spaces between words.

Left Margin

Entered as LMn where n is the number of spaces left blank for the left margin.

Defaults to 5 for WORDWISE and 0 for WORDWISE PLUS.

This embedded command is used to set the amount of space at the left margin. The value entered will denote the number of blank spaces you require at the beginning of each line. This command will not alter the line length in any way, but by making the left margin larger it will move the printed text on the paper to the right.

Line Length

Entered as LLn where n is the value of the number of characters required in the line length.

Defaults to 70.

This embedded command is used to stipulate the number of characters to be printed in one line across the page. When in Edit Mode the text on the screen is 40 characters across and will change to the line length when in Preview Mode (*see* previewing text on page 67). The line length should be set with the size of paper, type of printer and left margin in mind. If a left margin is set at 15 and a line length of 80, then there will be 15 spaces for the margin followed by 80 characters of text on the line, making a total of 95 characters. On some printer paper this would be too large.

Line Number End +

Entered as LNE.

This embedded command will turn off the line numbering and should be used in conjunction with LNS. *See* LNS for further details.

Line Number Start +

Entered as LNS.

This embedded command is used to turn on the facility of numbering the lines while in Preview Mode. They will appear on the screen on the left side and will comprise of three digits. This facility is useful when you are using headers and footers and trying to position them into top and bottom space. As the line numbers take up spaces you may find that long lines of text will be continued on the next screen line (*see* previewing text, page 67).

Line Spacing

Entered as LSn where n is the value of the required spacing between the lines.

Defaults to single line spacing.

This embedded command is used when you wish to instruct the printer to use double or treble line spacing, i.e. double line spacing is a line of text, followed by a blank line, followed by a line of text etc.

No Justification

Entered as NJ.

Defaults to OFF.

This embedded command does the opposite of the Justify On command. Text will be printed with an uneven right margin. You can display your document with both styles by using these commands at the appropriate places.

Output Control code

Entered as OCn (or OCn,n if more than one number is required) where n is the value of the code required.

This embedded command is used to send output control codes to your printer. Different printers use different codes to achieve items such as underlining, condensed print etc. These codes are discussed in more detail on page 77. The red function keys can be programmed to operate the output control codes which will save time when keying in text (*see* page 50).

Pad Character definition

Entered as ¦ (default character), the key next to the left arrow (remember to use the <SHIFT>). This character will appear on the screen as two vertical lines.

This embedded command is used if you are justifying text and require certain groups of words or figures to be kept with a single space between. To obtain a straight right margin (justifying), the computer distributes the necessary extra spaces along the line. If there is a particular point where you do not want the extra spaces to be placed, this command is used. For example:

Edit Mode

> *f1JOf1LL45f2* 1st March 1984 is an
> example of the need to include a pad
> character that avoids the inclusion of
> extra spaces between the parts of the
> date when justifying.

Preview Mode

> 1st March 1984 is an example of the need to
> include a pad character that avoids the inclusion
> of extra spaces between the parts of the date when
> justifying.

Edit Mode

> *f1JOf1LL45f2* 1st || March || 1984 is an
> example of the need to include a
> character that avoids the inclusion of
> extra spaces between the parts of the
> date when justifying.

Preview Mode

> 1st March 1984 is an example of the need to
> include a pad character that avoids the inclusion
> of extra spaces between the parts of the date when
> justifying.

Page Length

Entered as PLn where n is the number of lines required on the page.

Defaults to 66.

This embedded command is used to set the number of lines on each page before starting the next. It can only be used in conjunction with the Enable Paging command. When setting the page length, the top and bottom spaces must be considered because these are subtracted from the page length to determine the number of lines of text. For example, *f1PL60f2* will actually give 48 lines of text because the Bottom Space and Top Space both default to 6 (*see* diagram).

```
1
2
3    Top Space defaults to 6
4
5
6
     Lines of text = 48
55
56
57   Bottom Space defaults to 6
58
59
60
```

Page Number

Entered as PN or PNn where n is the number of the page to be printed.

WORDWISE defaults to 1 if PN is entered.

WORDWISE PLUS defaults to centring 'Page 1' in the centre of the bottom space.

This embedded command is used to number your single sheets of paper, therefore Enable Paging is required. Once you have set the page number at the top of your document there is no need to type it in for every page, because WORDWISE will do it automatically for you. The embedded command to Print Page number is required if you are using WORDWISE. *See* Define Footer, Define Header and Centre if you wish to centre the page number.

Pause +

Entered as PA.

Defaults to OFF.

This embedded command is used if you require your printer to pause during printing. You may wish to change the golf-ball or daisy-wheel to give a different typeface, e.g. italics. To start the printer or previewing again you need to press the space bar.

Print File +

Entered as PF"name of file".

This embedded command is similar to the Get File command except the embedded commands are acted upon. However, if you use this command in the middle of your document, all later text will be affected by the commands contained in the file you call from disk or tape.

Print Page number

Entered as PP.

WORDWISE defaults to the Page Number.

WORDWISE PLUS defaults to printing the Page Number in the Bottom Space without having to key in this command.

This embedded command is used to place the position of the page number when printing out. For example:

*f1*DF*f1*PN*f1*PP*f2*<RETURN>

will print the page number as a footer on every page. *See* Define Footer on page 26.

*f1*DH*f1*PN*f1*PP*f2*<RETURN>

will print the page number as a header on every page. *See* Define Header on page 28.

Single Spacing

Entered as SS.

Defaults to ON.

This embedded command will instruct the printer to revert to single line spacing if previously you had used the command to alter the line spacing.

Space

Entered as SPn where n is the value of the number of lines that you wish to be left blank.

This embedded command is used if you wish a blank space to be left when you print out. You may require space to draw a diagram afterwards. For example:

*f1*SP10*f2*

will instruct the printer to leave 10 blank lines at that point in your text.

Temporary Indent

Entered as TIn where n is the value of the number of spaces you wish to indent.

This embedded command is used when you wish only that line of text to be indented, e.g. an indented paragraph. There is no need to cancel it because it is only a temporary command. The indentation will start on the next line if this command is entered in the middle of a line. For example:

Edit Mode

> *f1*TI5*f2* This paragraph will have its
> first line indented five spaces with
> subsequent lines blocked at the left
> margin.

Preview Mode

>   This paragraph will have its first line
> indented five spaces with subsequent lines blocked
> at the left margin.

Top Space

Entered as TSn where n is the value of the number of lines required in the top space.

Defaults to 6.

This embedded command sets the space which you require to be left blank at the top of each sheet, therefore you will need to use the Enable Paging command. This command must be considered with those of Page Length and Bottom Space. If you have a page length of 58, top space of 6 and bottom space of 6, then there will only be 46 lines of text on each page. The top and bottom spaces are added together and deducted from the page length (*see* the illustration below).

	1
	2
Top space	3
	4
	5
	6

Text 46 lines

	1
	2
Bottom space	3
	4
	5
	6

Underline End +

Entered as UE.

Defaults to Epson and related printers. Generates codes of 27,45,0.

This embedded command will turn off the underline facility on your printer. You must remember to turn off your underlining, otherwise the rest of your document will be underlined. *See* US command.

Underline Start +

Entered as US.

Defaults to Epson and related printers. Generates codes of 27,45,1.

This embedded command is used to turn on the underline facility on your printer. When previewing text it will appear, providing you are not using more than 80 columns across the page.

User-defined keys

The red function keys at the top of the keyboard can be used by WORDWISE in three ways:

(1) By pressing a red key to obtain a WORDWISE function.

(2) By pressing a red key while holding down a SHIFT key to activate a segment (WORDWISE PLUS only).

(3) By pressing a red key while holding down <CTRL> and <SHIFT>. This third method enables you to program the function keys to produce any codes you wish. For example, one key can be set up to produce one or more embedded commands, including the *f1* and *f2* effects.

In BASIC mode, type ∗KEY0||!!BP||!'' <RETURN> This programs function key zero with *f1* followed by BP for begin page, then *f2* to complete the usual sequence. The double vertical line is obtained by using <SHIFT> and the key next to the left-pointing arrow (cursor control) key. Exclamation and speech marks are obtained as usual. Now call up WORDWISE and obtain BP by simply holding down the <CTRL> and <SHIFT> keys with one hand, while pressing *f0* with the other.

   Pressing <BREAK> will not lose the new function key setting, but switching off the computer or pressing <CTRL> and <BREAK> will. To avoid typing in settings for all of the red keys each time you use WORDWISE, it is possible to prepare a program to do this for you. Use one of these two methods.

For disk users
Put a formatted disk into the drive and type the following when in BASIC mode:

∗BUILD !BOOT <RETURN>

You should obtain a line number 01 on the screen.
Continue typing the following list, pressing
<RETURN> after each complete line. Press
<ESCAPE> after you have RETURNed from the last
line. (Keys 11 to 15 are the COPY and arrowed keys,
which may also be redefined and used in the same
way. Leave out the lines programming keys 11 to 14
if you prefer to avoid using these extra keys.)

On line 1 type *FX18
On line 2 type *K.0||!||L||!#||!||M||!#||!'||!||L
etc.
*K.1||!!PL72||!!LL60||!!EM||!!EP||!!LM10||!''
*K.2||!!OC27,71||!''
*K.3||!!OC27,72||!''
*K.4||!!OC27,45,1||!''
*K.5||!!OC27,45,0||!''
*K.6||!!BP||!''
*K.7||!!TI5||!''
*K.8||!!IN10||!''
*K.9||!!CI||!''
*K.11||!!CE||!''
*K.12||!!GF'' ''||!''
*K.13||!!OC27,69,14||!''
*K.14||!!OC27,70,20||!''
*W.

(*Note:* when using key 12, position cursor under the
second GF speech mark before typing file name.)
   Those with the WORDWISE PLUS ROM can
substitute and add the following lines:

```
*K.2||!!DS||!''
*K.3||!!DE||!''
*K.4||!!US||!''
*K.5||!!UE||!''
*K.15||!!FI||!''
*W.
```

As you press <ESCAPE> the disk saves this file as
!BOOT. Now type *OPT4,3 <RETURN>; the disk
will rotate again before the !BOOT file is ready for
use. Use this disk in future to 'auto boot' by holding
down <SHIFT> and pressing, then releasing
<BREAK>. The file will load automatically and
WORDWISE will be ready for use with the extra
facilities. You should make a copy of the function key
strip in Figure 1 and insert this next to the
WORDWISE strip under the plastic.
(*Notes:* *K. is an abbreviated form of *KEY, keys 13
and 14 set up and disable enlarged-emphasized
print on Epson-compatible printers, *W. calls up
WORDWISE. Values for PL etc. can be changed to
suit your own requirements.)

For cassette users
Type in the following program and SAVE it to
cassette tape. It should then be CHAINed each time
the computer is switched on. (*Note:* the RETURN key
should only be pressed before each new numbered
line. NOT after each book line. REMarks need not be
typed in, e.g. line 15 can be omitted.)

```
10  *FX18
15  REM Line 10 clears the function keys
20  *K.0||!||L||!#||!||M||!#||!'||!||L
25  REM Key 0 Deletes a line
30  *K.1||!!PL72||!!LL60||!!EM||!!EP||!!LM10||!"
35  REM Key 1 gives Standard page, amend the
values if you wish
40  *K.2||!!OC27,71||!": REM Double Strike On
50  *K.3||!!OC27,72||!": REM Double Strike Off
60  *K.4||!!OC27,45,1||!": REM Underscore On
70  *K.5||!!OC27,45,0||!": REM Underscore Off
80  *K.6||!!BP||!"
90  *K.7||!!TI5||!": REM Temporary Indent, change
the value if you wish
100  *K.8||!!IN10||!": REM Indent Every Line until CI
110  *K.9||!!CI||!": REM Cancel Indent
120  REM Leave out lines 130,140,150,160, if you
125  REM wish to only program RED keys
130  *K.11||!!CE||!"
140  *K.12||!!GF" "||!": REM Put cursor under
second
145  REM speech mark when typing file name
150  *K.13||!!OC27,69,14||!": REM Enlarged
Emphasized Print On
160  *K.14||!!OC27,70,20||!": REM Enlarged
Emphasized Print Off
170  *W.: REM Calls up Wordwise
```

Those with the WORDWISE PLUS ROM can substitute and add the following lines:

```
40   *K.2||!!DS||!":REM Wordwise-Plus only
50   *K.3||!!DE||!"
60   *K.4||!!US||!"
70   *K.5||!!UE||!"
165  *K.15||!!FI||!": REM Fully Indent
```

Function key strips

Copy, from Figure 1 on page 56, the one you need and insert with the WORDWISE strip under the plastic.

Editing Text

Setting markers

One of the red function keys (*f3*) will set markers anywhere in your current document, to mark the beginning and end of a block of text. By setting markers you will be able to (1) copy marked text, (2) delete marked text, (3) move marked text, (4) save marked text, (5) preview marked text, (6) print marked text, (7) spool marked text. The marker appears on the screen as a white filled box.

Figure 1 *Function key strips*

WORDWISE `<CTRL> <SHIFT>`

f0	f1	f2	f3	f4	f5	f6	f7	f8	f9	←	→	↓	↑
Delete Line	Stand. Page	Double Strike On	Double Strike Off	Under-score On	Under-score Off	Begin Page	Temp. Indent	Indent	Cancel Indent	Centre	Get File	Enlar. Emph. On	Enlar. Emph. Off

↕ ¾ in (19 mm)

WORDWISE+ `<CTRL> <SHIFT>`

f0	f1	f2	f3	f4	f5	f6	f7	f8	f9	←	→	↓	↑	COPY
Delete Line	Stand. Page	Double Strike On	Double Strike Off	Under-score On	Under-score Off	Begin Page	Temp. Indent	Indent	Cancel Indent	Centre	Get File	Enlar. Emph. On	Enlar. Emph. Off	Fully Indent

Only two markers can be set at any one time. As you set a marker, a flashing block will appear on the right side of the status line and the computer will beep. If you try to set more than two markers, then a message will appear: 'MARKERS!' in the status line. This tells you that you will have to release them before you can set any more. When deleting and moving marked text the markers are released for you. To release the markers you delete them as you would a character (*see* page 14), or use the *f4* function key (*see* page 9) to search for them and then delete them as you would a character. If you are using WORDWISE PLUS, then <CTRL>**R** will release them automatically for you. Any embedded commands in a marked section will be copied, deleted, moved and saved at the same time. In some cases it might affect the rest of your document.

Copy marked text
This facility enables you to mark a section of text ready to copy it elsewhere. It remains in the original place as well as being copied to another position. If you had to prepare some compliment slips, it would be easier to type one and copy it several times, ready to print as one sheet for cutting up, than to print one out several times.

Type in your text and mark the section you require to be copied. Move the cursor to the position you wish it to be copied to. Press *f9*.

Type the example below and follow the instructions:

Edit Mode

```
■<RETURN>
  New Book Publishers<RETURN>
  162 New Street<RETURN>
  LONDON<RETURN><RETURN>
  With Compliments <RETURN>
_■
```

When the cursor is in the correct position, set markers by pressing *f3*. The blank line was placed at the beginning and marked as part of the text to copy to leave room between each compliment slip.

Place the cursor on the line after 'With Compliments'.

Press *f9* to copy marked text.

The markers remain in position should you wish to make further copies. If you do, then position the cursor where you want the copied text to be placed and press *f9*.

Delete marked text
See page 16.

Move marked text

When reading through your text you may wish to change the order in which it appears. Instead of deleting it and re-typing it, WORDWISE has the facility for you to move a marked section. The markers are released when you execute the move. The text to be moved must be marked by using *f3*. Place the cursor where you wish this marked text to be moved to and press *f8*. Remember, you may wish to move a blank line as well if you are moving paragraphs about.

Type the example below and follow the instructions:

Edit Mode

You must learn to move the cursor quickly about the document. ■The cursor is a small flashing line on the screen which shows you the printing point.■ The arrowed keys are auto-repeat keys.

Set markers as shown by pressing *f3*. The marked section is going to become the first sentence, therefore the two spaces after the full stop need to be moved as well.

Place the cursor at the beginning (the position you wish to move the text to).

Press *f8*. The sentence has moved and the resulting space has been closed up.

Save marked text

This option allows you to save part of your text onto disk or tape. It is necessary to place markers at the beginning and end of the text you wish to save. Go back to the main menu by pressing <ESCAPE>. Select option 3 and enter a document name <RETURN> (saving text is described in more detail on page 71). <ESCAPE> back to Edit Mode and you will see that your marked text and markers are still there as well as being saved. If you no longer require this marked section, then delete it by pressing *f7*.

Preview marked text

This facility enables you to preview your marked section of text only. This can save time if you have a long document and the changes you wish to make are on the last page. (*See* page 67 for more details on previewing text.) When you select the option to preview and there are markers in the text, the question 'Marked section only? (Y/N)' will appear. By answering Y for Yes, only the marked section will be previewed; answer N for No and the whole document will be previewed.

Print marked text

This option allows you to print only your marked section of text. (*See* page 78 for details of printing.) You might have a long document stored on disk or tape and need an extra copy of a certain page. To save the time and trouble of printing the whole document, you can just print the piece you require. When you select the print option the question 'Marked section only? (Y/N)' will appear. Answer Y for Yes and just the marked section will be printed; answer N for No and the whole of your document will be printed.

Spool marked text

See spool text on page 75. Mark the text in the usual way with markers, select option 8, answer yes to the question.

Case change

When typing in capital letters you are using upper case, and when typing in small letters you are using lower case. When reading through your text, you may wish to change a title from lower to upper case, which can be done without the need to delete it first and re-typing it. This is referred to as case change, and can be from upper to lower or vice versa. If when you first start you forget to turn off the CAPS LOCK, then use this facility.

The command for case change is <CTRL>**S**. Position the cursor underneath the letter you wish to change and press <CTRL>**S**. If you require more than one letter changed, then keep the key down. Try this example:

Edit Mode

| happy new year |

<CTRL>**S**

becomes

Edit Mode

| HAPPY NEW YEAR |

One problem you might encounter is when you try to change a word with an initial capital. The initial capital letter will change to lower case with the rest of the word in upper case. Try this example:

Edit Mode

| Wendy Chuter |

<CTRL>**S**

becomes

Edit Mode

| wENDY cHUTER |

but

Edit Mode

W<u>e</u>ndy Chuter

<CTRL>**S** four times

moves the cursor underneath the letter 'h'. <CTRL>**S**
to the end of the word becomes

Edit Mode

WENDY CHUTER

If you are changing a title from lower to upper case,
remember to omit changing those letters which are
already capitals.

Search and Replace

WORDWISE has a facility for you to search for a
word(s) and change it if you wish. When found, you
have the option of replacing it at every occurrence
throughout your document, or only in selected
places. Every occurrence is referred to as global
replacement, and in selected places as selective
replacement. The computer will only search
forwards from your positioning of the cursor; if your
cursor is at the end of your document, then nothing
will happen.

When selecting this option you will be asked to type in a search string and a replacement string. A string is a sequence of characters (including spaces). The search string is used to enable the computer to find the occurrence, and the replacement string is the substitute text. When searching for a string, the computer will be very logical. For instance, if you instructed it to search for the word 'the', it would also find such words as their, either, father etc., because these words all include the search string. To prevent this, enter a space before and after the search string so that it becomes <space> the <space>. The space either side of the word will prevent other occurrences in the middle of a word being found and possibly changed. Another point to remember when entering the search string is the use of capital letters. Searching for 'the' will not find the occurrence of 'The'. These points need noting because if you select global replacement you will not see what is replaced as it is done so quickly.

The facility is selected as Option 5 from the main menu. The following text and instructions are examples of selective replacement:

Edit Mode

```
Please order two blue teddy bears, eight
    blue balls and six blue cars.
```

In this instance, you wish to change the colour of the cars to red.

Position the cursor at the beginning of the text.

<ESCAPE> to Main Menu

Select Option 5 and a question will appear on the screen.

'Please enter search string'

Type blue <RETURN> and another question will appear.

'Please enter replacement string'

Type red <RETURN>

<ESCAPE> to Edit Mode

The cursor should now be flashing under the first occurrence of the word 'blue'.

'Replace? (Y/N)' is now flashing in the status line.

You do not want to replace this time, so type N for No. The cursor will now move to the next occurrence.

Answer **N** again.

This time the cursor is flashing beneath the occurrence you do wish to replace, so type Y for Yes.

The cursor would normally keep searching and asking about replacement until it reaches the end of the document.

Using the same text as at the beginning of selective replacement, here is an example of global replacement. In this instance, you wish to change the colour blue to red at every occurrence.

Position the cursor at the beginning of the text.

<ESCAPE> to the main menu

Select Option 5

'Please enter search string', in this case type blue
<RETURN>

'Please enter replacement string', in this case type
red <RETURN>

<ESCAPE> to Edit Mode

Notice that every occurrence of the word 'blue' has
now been changed to 'red'.

Word count to?

You may have to type a document of a certain length.
Displayed alongside 'Words' in the status line are
the number of words in your document from the start
to the end. Sometimes you may wish to know how
many words there are in a particular paragraph.
Position your cursor at the beginning of the
paragraph, press *f5* and then press RETURN. The
number of words in the status line should have
changed to show how many there are from the
cursor to the next occurrence of the RETURN key,
which will be at the end of the paragraph. By using
this facility the computer will lose the total number of
words in your document. To restore this, position the
cursor at the end of your document and insert a
character you have not previously used in your text,
e.g. % $ @. Now move your cursor to the beginning

of your document, press *f5* followed by the inserted character which you placed at the end of the document. Your word count will now be replaced with that for the whole of your document. If you go on keying in text, don't forget to delete the inserted character.

Previewing text

Before committing your text to paper, by printing out, you can preview your work. In Edit Mode there are only 40 characters across the screen and the embedded commands are not acted upon. When previewing you will be able to see exactly how your document will be printed out. The embedded commands are acted upon and any page breaks are shown, if you have used the necessary commands. You may wish to change the layout or even begin a page in a different place. This can all be done and seen before committing your work to paper. Only if you use WORDWISE PLUS will you see the embedded commands for underline and double strike in Preview Mode.

    When previewing text, the screen will show up to 80 characters across the screen. This includes any space put in for the left margin. By setting a line length of 80 and a left margin of 20 it would make previewing difficult: you are asking for 100 characters across. The screen will show this by placing the extra characters on a separate line, but this is not how your document will appear on paper.

If you omit the embedded command for the left margin, you would then be able to preview your text as it will look when printed out. Once you have previewed it, type in the command for the left margin. All this command will do is move the text across the paper to the right.

Another point to remember is that Preview Mode takes up a lot of the computer's memory. Once the 'Characters free' in the status line reaches about 15500, then your text will be previewed in 40 characters across. If you wish to see your text previewed when less than these characters are free, then save it in smaller parts. If your computer has been fitted with a memory extension, then this will not be necessary. I would suggest that you always preview your text before printing.

To preview text you need to select Option 7 from the main menu. As soon as you press number 7, your text will flash onto the screen in Preview Mode. If your document is more than 23 lines in depth, then the top part of it will quickly scroll off the top of the screen. To prevent this happening, press <CTRL> and <SHIFT> together as soon after the number 7 as you can, which will stop the document from scrolling.

To resume, just release the <CTRL> and <SHIFT> and use them again if further stoppages are required. If you have used the embedded commands EP and EM the computer will stop automatically at the end of each page. Pressing the <SPACE BAR> will enable you to preview the next page. If you are using WORDWISE PLUS you can use the <SPACE BAR> to stop and start the scrolling. If at any time you wish to stop previewing (to return to Edit Mode to make a change), then press <ESCAPE> twice and you will return to Edit Mode.

Follow these instructions for previewing text:

Edit Mode
Key in some text (maybe a passage from this book) and place some different embedded commands in it. I suggest that you use EM and EP.

Proof-read it and correct any typing and spelling errors.

<ESCAPE> to Main Menu
Preview your text by selecting Option 7. Remember to hold <CTRL> and <SHIFT> down immediately afterwards.

When you reach the bottom of your document, the message 'press any key' will appear. By doing this, it will take you back to the main menu.

At this point you can, if satisfied with your text, save it or print it out.

If you wish to change anything, then <ESCAPE> twice and you will return to Edit Mode.

Try changing some of the embedded commands and then preview again.

Storage and Retrieval

Using disks

When you first purchase a disk, it will need formatting. A utility disk for this purpose will have been provided with your disk drive, along with the necessary instructions.

You can obtain single-or double-sided disks, your choice depending on whether you possess a single- or double-sided drive. For normal usage, a single-density disk is sufficient.

Care must be taken when handling a disk. Do not touch the magnetized surface of the disk inside the black cover; handle it by the label. Observe the guidelines usually printed on the reverse of the outer envelope concerning storage. In particular, keep disks away from magnetic fields and heat sources.

Avoid using the disk commands *BACKUP, *COMPACT and *COPY unless you have saved your current document first. These commands destroy anything in the current memory. You can, however, use the commands *CAT, *INFO and *DELETE without affecting your current document in memory.

Saving

When using the computer, you are using the part of memory which is volatile. In other words, when you press the BREAK key or switch the computer off, all your text may be lost. If there is a document you wish to keep for future use, you can save it onto disk or tape. At a later date you can load it in again and continue work on it. If you are typing a long document, I would suggest that you save it occasionally in case you accidentally lose it (*see also* saving marked text on page 60).

Care should be taken when saving a document. You will be asked to enter a filename which is the name you wish to call your document. If you enter one that has already been used, the computer will overwrite the original on the disk with the new version. The BBC computer will only allow you to use a filename up to 7 characters in length, and only 31 filenames can be catered for on a disk.

When you have created text, you will need to save it all. I would suggest that you do this before printing because it has been known for a printer to malfunction, and you might lose your text. When you are satisfied with your final layout, <ESCAPE> from Edit Mode to the main menu.

Disk users
From the main menu, select Option 1 and the question 'Please enter filename' will appear.

Enter the name of the document, bearing in mind what will happen if you use an existing filename. Press <RETURN> and the disk drive will start.

71

After the completion of saving, the option will stop flashing and the main menu will still be displayed on the screen.

It is possible to see if it has been stored on the disk. Type *INFO (the name of your document) <RETURN>. Displayed upon the screen will be information, such as where it is stored on the disk and how much space it takes up.

As well as being stored on the disk, it still remains in the computer's memory until you delete it, load in another file or switch the computer off. From the main menu, press <ESCAPE> and you will see that the document is still there.

Cassette users
Follow the same procedure until you enter the filename. After pressing <RETURN> on the screen, the statement 'RECORD then RETURN' will appear. This instruction tells you to place your tape in the data recorder, press the RECORD and PLAY buttons together on the recorder, and then press <RETURN> on the computer. Again, when the text has been recorded on the tape, the option will stop flashing. Check to see that it has recorded correctly by re-winding the tape to the position you started recording at and typing *CAT.

WORDWISE PLUS

When saving you will be shown on the screen the name of the last filename that was used by you since switching on the computer. This is to help you when you wish to save the text under another filename, and not overwrite the one being held on the disk. If you choose the same name as one already used on the disk, then the question 'Replace old file? (Y/N) will appear on the screen. If you answer yes, the text on the disk is overwritten with the text presently in the computer's memory; if you answer no, the statement 'File NOT saved!' will appear. This gives you the opportunity to change the filename.

Loading text

Any text which has been saved onto disk or tape can be loaded back into the computer's memory. There are two options available to you: (i) load new text; or (ii) load text to cursor.

Load new text
If you load new text you must be careful because it will destroy any text currently held in the computer's memory.

From the main menu, select Option 2. The question 'Please enter filename' will appear.

Type in the filename of the text as it appears on the catalogue of the disk. If the question 'No such file!' appears on the screen, you have either typed the filename incorrectly or the wrong disk is in the disk drive. After entering the filename, press <RETURN>.

When the loading has been completed, the option on the main menu will stop flashing.

Press <ESCAPE> to Edit Mode and your document should now be displayed upon the screen.

Tape users
If you are using tape, enter the filename, <RETURN>, press PLAY on the recorder.

Load text to cursor
The option of loading text to cursor will allow you to merge text from different filenames.

While in Edit Mode, position the cursor where you wish the merged text to begin.

<ESCAPE> to the main menu and select Option 4. Make sure that you have the disk containing the file you wish to merge in the disk drive (or tape in the recorder).

A statement will appear, 'Please enter filename'. Type in the name of the file you wish to merge and press <RETURN>. The text will now be loaded into the computer's memory without destroying your current text.

<ESCAPE> to Edit Mode to confirm that it has been displayed at the required position.

WORDWISE PLUS
If you have already saved or loaded other documents since switching on the computer, you will see the question 'Are you sure? (Y/N)' on the screen.

This is a safety precaution against either the wrong selection of an option from the main menu or to remind you that you will lose your current document when you load in a new one. Answer y for yes and proceed as for loading text. Answer n for no and the option you selected will be ignored. The main menu will be displayed for your next choice.

Spool text

This option allows you to save your text in such a way that it can be recalled on a computer which has not been fitted with a WORDWISE chip. It is stored as an ASCII file which can then be called from BASIC. I suggest that you remove the embedded commands before saving, otherwise it is difficult to read when it contains the ASCII equivalents of the embedded commands. This facility could be used if you wish to send a document on disk, tape or electronic mail. From disk or tape, the document can be *TYPEd by the receiver. Follow these instructions to spool text.

Key in your text without any embedded commands. I suggest you save it as a WORDWISE document as a precaution against accidental loss.

From the main menu, select Option 8.

Give the document a filename<RETURN>. Use a different one to any already used, otherwise your previously saved text under this filename will be overwritten as an ASCII file.

Your work will now be stored as an ASCII document. If you <CTRL>**BREAK** from WORDWISE and then *TYPE "your document name"<RETURN> you should see your text appear on the screen. Holding <CTRL> and <SHIFT> together will stop it from scrolling too quickly.

Printers

Printers are used to obtain a 'hard copy' of your work. The printer is connected to the computer in one of two ways: a parallel printer is connected underneath the computer by means of a wide ribbon cable; a serial printer is connected at the back of the computer in the socket marked RS423 and uses a 5-DIN plug. The BBC defaults to a parallel printer.

If you are using a serial printer with the BBC, then it is necessary to enter the following before printing:

*FX5,2<RETURN>   to tell the computer you are using the serial interface.
*FX6,0   will cause your printer to line feed when it receives a carriage return. This should be entered after *FX5,2.
*FX8,n   (where n is the baud rate which should be mentioned in your printer manual) to tell the computer the speed at which data can be sent from the computer to the printer. Refer to page 407 of the *User Guide* supplied with the computer for a list of the baud rates.

In your printer manual there are instructions on how to set the DIP (internal selector) switches. These switches can be used to control such things as automatic line feed at each carriage return. If your printer does not line feed automatically, and you do not wish to take the cover off the printer to reset the switches, typing *FX6<RETURN> before attempting to print out will correct this.

Also from your printer manual you will find the control codes for such items as underlining and condensed print. On page 486 of the BBC *User Guide* there is a table of ASCII codes. For example, if your printer manual instructs you to use ESC G to start underlining, this converts to the embedded command OC27,71. On the BBC micro, the value 27 represents ESCAPE, the 71 will be found in the ASCII table already mentioned to represent the letter G. You should note that there are different ASCII values for upper and lower case letters.

Terminology used

Bi-directional — a printer that is capable of printing from left to right and right to left. It prints a line in reverse order when printing from right to left.
Continuous paper — this is fan-fold paper with holes at the side. It comes as one large batch of paper similar to a kitchen roll with perforated ends of sheets should you require to tear some off.
CPS — characters per second — the rate at which the printer can print out.

Daisy-wheel — a type of print head which has the characters at the end of a wheel. They are struck by a small hammer which results in the character appearing on the paper.

Dot-matrix — a type of print head which forms the character by using dots. This does not usually give a letter-quality print.

Friction-feed — this facility on a printer will enable you to use single sheets of paper.

Golf-ball — a type of print head shaped like a golf-ball with the characters on it. It will revolve round to give the different characters.

Logic-seeking — the print head when starting a new line will move to the first character, and not back to the margin.

Pitch — the number of characters across to 1 inch, e.g. 10 pitch=10 characters to 1 in, 12 pitch=12 characters to 1 in.

Tractor or sprocket feed — this facility on a printer requires the paper to have holes at the side, in order to feed the paper through the printer to start new lines.

Uni-directional — a printer that has to return to the beginning of the left margin to type each new line.

Printing

After correcting any errors and previewing your text you may wish to print a copy of your work. Make sure your printer is connected to the computer and that it is switched to 'on line'. *See* page 76 for further details about printers. Place some paper into the printer.

From the main menu, select Option 6 to print text. All your text in the memory of the computer will now be printed out. If you have not used the embedded command EP (Enable Paging), then all of your document will be printed out without stopping. If you have used this command, the printer will stop at the end of each page to enable you to place a new sheet of paper in the printer. Once you have done this, press the space bar on the computer to continue printing. At the end of printing you will be asked to press any key, which will return you to the main menu. Your text, however, is still in the computer's memory should you wish to continue work on it. You have the facility to print only the marked section, which is explained on page 61.

WORDWISE PLUS
You are able to instruct the computer to print a document a number of times. To do this you have to place a procedure into any one of the segments (*see* page 82 for further details about using segments).

From the main menu, select Option 9 Segment Menu. Select a segment (in this example, I have assumed you selected segment 0) and type in the following:

SELECT TEXT<RETURN>
DOTHIS<RETURN>
PRINT TEXT<RETURN>
TIMES 2<RETURN>

The figure in the last line is the number of copies you require. You can use any figure. This small procedure could be saved on disk or tape and loaded into a segment when required. The figure can be changed by using the DELETE key to obtain the required number of copies.

<ESCAPE> to the Segment Menu. Select Option 9 to return to the main menu. Make sure you have paper in your printer. Press <SHIFT> and *f0* together. Your document should start to print out the number of times required.

Segments (WORDWISE PLUS Only)

WORDWISE PLUS has been designed so that you can split the computer's memory up into segments. You can use up to 10 segments, numbered from 0–9, as well as the main text area. This enables different documents or programs to be held in the computer's memory simultaneously. You can work on any of these documents providing there is sufficient room in the whole of the computer's memory. The memory is not divided into exact divisions for each segment, it adapts to the size of each document. Obviously the more segments you use, the less room there is for the main text.

The segments can be used as notepads. You can try out a style of display, or type in some text which needs to be sorted alphabetically, and then the work can be copied over into the main text or from one segment to another (*see* inserting text from a segment, page 13). You can switch from the main text

area to a segment at any time, or from one segment
to another, via a menu. Supplied with the package is
a tape containing examples of text and some special
programs such as Mail Merge and the alphabetical
sorting of names. I suggest that if you are using a
disk drive, you copy the material from tape to disk
before experimenting.

You will not be able to use the Search and Replace
or Spool facilities when working in a segment. To use
a segment, you will have to choose Option 9 from the
main menu. When you have done this, the Segment
Menu will be displayed upon the screen.

The Segment Menu

```
SEGMENT MENU

1)  Save segment
2)  Load segment
3)  Save marked text
4)  Load text to cursor
5)  Select segment (0)
6)  Print segment
7)  Preview segment
8)  Delete segment
9)  Main menu

ESC Edit Mode

Please enter choice_
```

Options 1, 2, 3, 4, 6, 7 are the same as the main menu options except they relate to saving or loading from the numbered segment.

Select segment

Option 5 allows you to change the segment number that you will be able to work in. When you first switch on, the segment number defaults to 0. You can see which segment you are working on by the number displayed alongside Option 5.

Select Option **5**
Which segment ? (0–9)_
Type **1**

Notice that the number alongside Option 5 has now changed to 1. This shows that you are now working in segment 1.

<ESCAPE> to SEG 1 Edit Mode

Delete segment

When you have finished with a segment and you do not require it any more, it is possible to delete the text in that segment without having to set markers for deleting text.

Make sure that the number alongside Option 5 is the correct number of the segment that you wish to delete. If it is not, then change it using Option 5.

From the Segment Menu, choose Option 8.

'Are you sure ? (Y/N)
Y

<ESCAPE> will prove to you that the text has been deleted.

Returning to the main menu

When you wish to return to the main text area, you will have to select Option 9 from the Segment Menu.
  Select Option 9.
  Main menu will now appear on the screen.
  <ESCAPE> to Edit Mode.

Segment Applications

Mail Merge

This facility will allow you to send the same letter to several people, but with individual addresses at the top.

(1) Load MAIL1 into Segment 0. (This is one of the programs on the WORDWISE PLUS tape.)
(2) <ESCAPE> to Edit Mode. Find line 3 in the program and alter the name of the address file to ADRDATA, if you intend using that demonstration file rather than creating your own, i.e. line 3 becomes A%=OPENIN"ADRDATA" <ESCAPE>
(3) Select Option 9 for the main menu.

(4) <ESCAPE> to create the letter below:

f1EPf1EMf2

26 August 1985

Dear Sir

Thank you for your completed application form. Please could you telephone to confirm your interview time.

Yours faithfully *f1BPf2*

(5) Move the cursor to the start of the document.
(6) <SHIFT> **f0** to activate the program in Segment 0. (*Note:* If you are using tape, wind it to just before the start of the ADRDATA file before activating the segment.)
(7) Switch your printer on line if necessary.
(8) The letter prints out with the first address from the ADRDATA file at the top. (You can, of course, create your own address file — but be sure to leave a blank line between each address, and to change line 3 of the MAIL1 program to accept the name of your own file. However, if you call your list 'ADDRESS', the MAIL1 program is already programmed to accept that name.)

Problems
The MAIL1 program as given on the tape causes two problems. Firstly, a page number is printed at the foot of each letter. Secondly, the program prints the address above the date — it should, of course, usually go after the date.

I therefore list below suggested alterations to the MAIL1 program to overcome these two problems. To amend your program, load MAIL1 into main text area and <ESCAPE> to Edit Mode.

Look for line 11 in the program. It says CURSOR TOP Position the cursor at the beginning of the line below this (FKEY 3)
<RETURN> to create a blank line
In this blank line type the command CURSOR DOWN 2
Now look for line 21. It says TIMES 500
Beneath this line add the extra line Z%=GET
<ESCAPE> to menu

SAVE this amended program as MAIL3 on your tape or disk. You should then load this program into a segment when you require to use the mail merge facility with my suggested alterations. When you type the letter this time, omit the embedded commands EP, EM and BP. Place any commands of your own on the date line. When you have typed the date, <RETURN> three times. After printing each letter the program will cause the print out to stop. Remove your first letter and insert the paper for the next. Press any key (except BREAK) to continue printing.

When you construct your own address file, I suggest that you store the female names in a separate file, e.g. 'ADDFEM', so that you are able to change the salutation (Dear Madam). An alternative method is to amend the program still further! Compare the revised program below with your version and SAVE the new version as MAIL5.

```
REM "MAIL1" with alterations

CLOSE#0
A%=OPENIN"ADDRESS"
SELECT TEXT
DELETE MARKERS
CURSOR TOP
FKEY 3
FKEY 3
REPEAT
  B$=GLF$#A%
  FKEY 7
  CURSOR TOP
  CURSOR DOWN 2
  FKEY 3
  REPEAT
    A$=GLF$#A%
    IF A$<>"" THEN PROCinsert
  UNTIL A$=""
  TYPE " R"
  TYPE "Dear "
  TYPE B$+" R"+" R"
  FKEY 3
  PRINT TEXT
  DOTHIS
  TIMES 500
  Z%=GET
UNTIL EOF#A%
P. ".......FINISHED......."
A%=GET
GOTO END
.insert
TYPE A$+" R"
ENDPROC
```

```
.END
CLOSE#0
DISPLAY
```

Now create a list of names and addresses in the form of the sample list below. The first line must contain the name as you wish it to appear in the salutation, e.g. Fred it you want that letter to start with Dear Fred. The second line should contain the name as it will appear in the address. Place a blank line as usual between each new address. SAVE this under the filename "ADDRESS".

Mr Andrews
Mr A B Andrews
23 Oakshott Gardens
Portsmouth

Mrs Williams
Mrs W C Williams
19 Further Road
Reading

Mr Smith
Mr A T Smith
22 Wordsworth Avenue
Bournemouth

Now type your letter with the date on the first line, followed by <RETURN> twice. Do not type a salutation, but type the first line of your first paragraph. Now proceed as before.

MAIL2

If you wish to use this version of the mail merge program, which calls the addresses from a segment rather than from a file, similar changes can be made to the program. SAVE this as MAIL4. (*Note* that you should use Segment 9 to store your list of addresses.)

Alphabetical sorting

Another program contained on the WORDWISE PLUS tape sorts items alphabetically or numerically. If you are working on a document which requires items to be typed in alphabetical order, you can use this program to do it for you. The text is sorted by the first letters or numbers in each line. The names given on the tape have been typed with the christian names first, therefore the list is sorted into alphabetical order of the christian names. It is usual to sort into alphabetical order of surnames; it is therefore important to remember to key in the surnames first. If you are in the middle of using the main text for your work, then it is possible to use a segment to sort the names and then to copy them across into your main text afterwards. Follow through these instructions:

(1) Load the program 'NAMSORT' into a segment.
(2) Type in your list of names in a segment or the main text area if you are not using this. Put each name on a separate line by pressing <RETURN> after each one. Insert a <RETURN> at the end of your list or the program will not work.
(3) <ESCAPE> to the menu.

(4) Press <SHIFT> and the number of the segment you loaded the 'NAMSORT' program into.

(5) Wait a few seconds and you will see the names appear on the screen in alphabetical order.

(6) If you used a segment for the sorting procedure, then copy your sorted text into your main text (*see* inserting from a segment).

It is also possible to sort a list of names and addresses. Key in the list, remembering to insert a <RETURN> between each new name and address, but not between a name and its own address. Follow the same instructions as above. The names will be sorted in alphabetical order according to the first letter in the first line.

Continuous processing

(Only suitable for disk users.)

When you are working on a long document, it may be necessary to split it into several smaller documents because of the limiting size of memory available. There are four programs on the tape that enable you to print out any number of these as one long document. You may find it necessary to insert one or more <RETURN>s at the beginning of each of the smaller documents, if you require to indicate a break in the text between one document and the next as it is printed. The embedded commands that you use at the beginning of the first document will determine the printing parameters throughout. For example, EM EP at the beginning of the first page will cause the printer to pause for single sheets and number them sequentially. It is therefore unnecessary to use these embedded commands at the beginning of each new document.

Follow these instructions:

(1) Load Segment 2 with PDOC.
(2) Load Segment 9 with INITCON.
(3) Create in Segment 6 a list of the document names in the order you intend printing (it is necessary for them to be on the same disk, as must also be the programs CONTIN1 and CONTIN2).
(4) SAVE this list as FLIST.
(5) Place paper in the printer and switch it on line.
(6) <SHIFT> *f2* to activate process.

Two-column print out

It is possible to use the DUALCOL program on the tape provided with the WORDWISE PLUS ROM to print out text in two columns. To avoid altering the program as given, it is necessary to follow the instructions stated below.

However, your tape may contain some errors in the DUALCOL program. To check if your version has been updated, load DUALCOL into main text or segment and look at the 17th line up from the bottom; if it reads REPEAT G% then change it to DOTHIS. The 15th line up from the bottom may read AGAIN; if it does, change it to TIMES G%.

(1) Load some text (or type some) into the main text area. Remove any embedded commands that set formatting parameters (e.g. take out page length, line length and margin commands — but leave in Double Strike and similar commands).

(2) Put in embedded commands to set a line length of 33 and justification on.

(3) <ESCAPE> to main menu and select Option 8 to Spool Text. Give your spooled file a new name, not one that is already in use.

(4) Select the Segment Menu and load the DUALCOL program into segment 0. <ESCAPE> to Edit Mode and look for the line C$="DOCUMENT" (line 15). Change this to the name of your own spooled file.

(5) Delete the *FX6,0 command in line 12 if your printer is already set for automatic line feed, i.e. it usually winds on to the next line by itself.

(6) <ESCAPE> to menu and check that your printer is switched on line with paper loaded.

(7) Activate the DUALCOL program by <SHIFT> *f0*.

Indexing

This facility could help you to create an index. The computer is instructed to search for a given string and then report to you the page numbers of these occurrences. Remember that the computer will only locate the exact search string. For example, when indexing this book, if I wanted to find every mention of inserting, I would also have to look for insert. A program is loaded into one segment and the search strings into another.

   Follow these instructions:

(1) Load into the main text area the document you wish to index.
(2) Load into Segment 0 the program DOINDEX.
(3) Load into Segment 1 the program INDEX.
(4a) Enter into Segment 7 the search strings you require.

or

(4b) Search through your main text area and place the cursor beneath the first letter of any word you wish to include in your index. <SHIFT>*f0* will use the DOINDEX program to place that word automatically into Segment 7. Continue in this way.
(5) <ESCAPE> to menu.
(6) <SHIFT>*f1* to activate the program. The screen will go blank while it is searching. When it has finished, the segment menu will appear on the screen, showing that segment 8 is being used. This is where you will find your list of word strings with their page occurrences.
(7) <ESCAPE> to Edit Mode of Segment 8.

Summary of Embedded Commands

Command	Function	Defaults to
BP	Begin Page	
BS	Bottom space	6 lines
CE	Centre	1 line centred
CI	Cancel Indent	
CO	Continuous Output	ON
CP	Continuous Paging	
DE +	Double strike End	Code 27,72
DF	Define Footing	Line 3
DF +	Define Footing	Page Number
DH	Define Heading	Line 3
DM	Disable Message	ON
DP	Define Pound sign	Code 96
DS +	Double strike Start	Code 27,71
DT	Define Tab stop	10,20,30 etc.
EM	Enable 'Paper' Message	No message
EP	Enable Paging	OFF
FI +	Fully Indent	
FP	Footing Position	Line 3
GF	Get File	
HP	Heading Position	Line 3
IN	Indent	0
JO	Justification On	ON
X JO +	Justification On	OFF

LL	Line Length	70 characters
LM	Left Margin	5
LM +	Left Margin	0
LNE +	Line Number End	
LNS +	Line Number Start	
LS	Line Spacing	Single line
NJ	No Justification	OFF
✗ NJ +	No Justification	ON
OC	Output Control code	
PA +	Pause	OFF
PC	Pad character	‖ on screen
PF +	Print File	
PL	Page Length	66 lines
PN	Page Number	number 1
PP	Print Page number	Page Number
SP	Space	0
SS	Single Spacing	ON
TI	Temporary Indent	0
TS	Top Space	6
UE +	Underline End	Code 27,45,0
US +	Underline Start	Code 27,45,1

Summary of Cursor Movements

→	will move the cursor one character to the right
←	will move the cursor one character to the left
↑	will move the cursor one line up
↓	will move the cursor one line down
\<CTRL\> and →	will move the cursor one word to the right
\<CTRL\> and ←	will move the cursor one word to the left
\<CTRL\> and ↑	will move the cursor up one screenful (23 lines)
\<CTRL\> and ↓	will move the cursor down one screenful
\<SHIFT\> and →	will move the cursor to the right end of line
\<SHIFT\> and ←	will move the cursor to the left end of line
\<SHIFT\> and ↑	will move the cursor to start of the text
\<SHIFT\> and ↓	will move the cursor to end of the text
f4 and (a character, e.g. \<RETURN\>, *f1*, *f2*, full stop, comma)	will move the cursor to the next occurrence of that character

Summary of the Function Keys

f0   switches on/off the overwrite mode
f1   used to start the embedded commands
f2   used to end the embedded commands
f3   sets a marker
f4   will move the cursor to a particular character
f5   used to calculate the number of words in a
     particular part of the document
f6   will delete text from the current cursor position,
     to the next occurrence of the character entered
     after pressing f6
f7   will delete marked text
f8   will move marked text
f9   will copy marked text

Summary of CTRL and SHIFT Commands

\<CTRL\> and A	will delete the character underneath the cursor
\<CTRL\> and D	will delete the word underneath the cursor
\<CTRL\> and R	will delete the markers (+ only)
\<CTRL\> and S	will change the case of the letter
\<CTRL\> and →	will move the cursor one word to the right
\<CTRL\> and ←	will move the cursor one word to the left
\<CTRL\> and ↑	will move the cursor up 23 lines
\<CTRL\> and ↓	will move the cursor down 23 lines
\<SHIFT\> and →	will move the cursor to the right end of the line
\<SHIFT\> and ←	will move the cursor to the left end of the line
\<SHIFT\> and ↑	will move the cursor to the start of the text
\<SHIFT\> and ↓	will move the cursor to the end of the text
\<SHIFT\> and *f0*	will activate the program in segment 0
\<CTRL\> \<SHIFT\> and a function key	will produce the code programmed for that key
\<CTRL\> \<BREAK\>	will cancel the WORDWISE command and enable you to use the computer in BASIC

Specimen Document of Embedded Commands

This specimen document will show you Edit Mode with embedded commands entered. In the following section you will be able to see how it has been printed out.

*f1*LL50*f1*PL47*f1*EM*f1*EP*f1*LNS*f1*LM20*f2*
*f1*DF*f1*PP*f2*<RETURN>

*f1*DH*f1*CE*f2* 1st January 1985<RETURN>

*f1*CE*f2*‖*f1*OC27,45,1*f2* EXAMPLE DOCUMENT *f1*OC27,45,0*f2*

or

*f1*CE*f2*‖*f1*US*f2* EXAMPLE DOCUMENT *f1*UE*f2*

The first title shows you the commands necessary to centre and underline a heading using WORDWISE. A pad character has been entered between the Centre and Output Control codes to ensure the underline is only under the centred headings. The second Output Control code will end the underline.

The second title shows you the commands necessary to centre and underline a heading using WORDWISE PLUS.

The Line Length has been set at 50. The Page Length has been set at 47, and Enable Message and Enable Paging for single sheets of paper. The Line Number Start command (+ only) will turn on the numbering of the lines while in Preview Mode. The Left Margin has been set at 20. The Define Footer and Print Page will instruct the printer to print the page number at the left margin. The Define Header will print 1st January 1985 in the centre of the top space of every page.

*f1*JO*f2*   This document demonstrates the embedded commands as they appear in Edit Mode. The resulting print out will be shown on page 101. The first paragraph has been justified by using the JO command at the beginning. *f1*NJ*f2*

*f1*TI5*f2*   The rest of the document will not be justified because NJ has been inserted at the end of the paragraph. This paragraph has the first line indented 5 spaces as TI5 is placed at the beginning. This is a temporary indent and will not affect subsequent lines.

*f1*IN5*f2*   All text is now indented 5 spaces; a CI command is required to cancel this. *f1*CI*f2*

*f1*PF"Para1"*f2* (+ only)

*f1*SP5*f2*   will instruct the printer to leave 5 line spaces.

*f1*BP*f2*   will force a page break at this position.

*f1*LS2*f2*   If you require your text to be printed in double line spacing, then enter the command for Line Spacing. *f1*SS*f2* (or *f1*LS1*f2*) will change the Line Spacing back to single line spacing. Notice that as the command has been entered in the mid-line it will not be effected until the next line.

*f1*OC27,71*f2*   Tabulation   *f1*OC27,72*f2*

or

*f1*DS*f2*   Tabulation   *f1*DE*f2*

This heading will be printed in Double Strike mode.

*f1*DT25,31,37*f2*   will Define Tab stops at these numbered positions.

Edit Mode
→ abc → abc → abc <RETURN>
→ def → def →def

Preview Mode

	abc	abc	abc
	def	def	def

*f1*BP   will ensure that the final footer is printed.

1st January 1985

EXAMPLE DOCUMENT

or

EXAMPLE DOCUMENT

The first title shows you the commands necessary to centre and underline a heading using WORDWISE. A pad character has been entered between the Centre and Output Control codes to ensure the underline is only under the centred headings. The second Output Control code will end the underline.

The second title shows you the commands necessary to centre and underline a heading using WORDWISE PLUS.

The Line Length has been set at 50. The Page Length has been set at 47, and Enable Message and Enable Paging for single sheets of paper. The Line Number Start command (+ only) will turn on the numbering of the lines while in Preview Mode. The Left Margin has been set at 20. The Define Footer and Print Page will instruct the printer to print the page number at the left margin. The Define Header will print 1st January 1985 in the centre of the top space of every page.

This document demonstrates the embedded commands as they appear in Edit Mode. The resulting print out will be as shown on page 98. The first paragraph has been justified by using the JO command at the beginning.

101

The rest of the document will not be justified because NJ has been inserted at the end of the first paragraph. This paragraph has the first line indented 5 spaces as TI5 is placed at the beginning. This is a temporary indent and will not affect subsequent lines.

All text is now indented 5 spaces, a CI command is required to cancel this.

This command will Print a File that might contain standard paragraphs, insert the file into the text and thus prevent the need to type them in each time.

will instruct the printer to leave 5 line spaces.

2

will force a page break at this position.

If you require your text to be printed in double

line spacing then enter the command for Line

Spacing. *f1SSf2* (or *f1LS1f2*) will change the Line
Spacing back to single line spacing. Notice that as
the command has been entered in the mid-line it will
not be effected until the next line.

Tabulation

or

Tabulation

This heading will be printed in Double Strike mode.

will Define Tab stops at these numbered positions.

Edit Mode
    abc abc abc<RETURN>
    def def def

Preview Mode

	abc	abc	abc
	def	def	def

will ensure that the final footer is printed.

3

Problems

When you switch on, WORDWISE is displayed upon the screen
This means that the ROM chip has been fitted incorrectly. It will still function but it is better to start from BASIC and call up WORDWISE.

The status line is not visible on the screen
To move the display down, type *TV 255 <RETURN> while the menu is on the screen. *See* page 4.

Lines do not wordwrap properly, i.e. there are large gaps at the end of the right margin where it is possible to fit the next word
This may be caused when making corrections to your text while in Edit Mode. By moving the cursor up or down a few lines, this will be corrected. *See* page 7.

The specified character is not found when using f4
The cursor will only search from the current cursor position onwards. Make sure your cursor is positioned at the beginning of the text. Alternatively, the specified character may not exist in the text. *See* page 9.

When inserting previously saved text, nothing happens
Have you placed the disk containing the required text in the disk drive, or have you rewound the tape to just before the start of the required file? Make sure you select Option 4 and not Option 2. *See* page 12.

Text is not inserted correctly from a segment into the main text
Did you position the cursor in the main text at the correct position?

Did you type :TYPE SEGMENT n<RETURN> ?

Did you use the correct segment number? *See* page 13.

Losing some of your text while in overwrite mode
Due to your forgetting to change back to Insert Mode after you have overwritten your required text.

An embedded command is not acted upon
Did you use *f1* before and *f2* after the embedded command?

If the embedded commands take up more than one line of text, some of them may not be acted upon.

Did you place *f1* between the commands on the same line, with *f2* at the end?

Check that an *f1* or *f2* has not been accidentally deleted when correcting text.

The footer is not printed out on the last page of your document
*f1*BP needs to be entered at the end of the text to instruct the printer to print the last footer. *See* page 28.

The first line on a continuation sheet does not start in the correct place
*f1*BP*f2* is acted upon immediately, therefore if there is a <RETURN> after it, the printer will place a blank line at the top of your continuation sheet. It may be necessary to have the end of one page and the start of the next on the same line while in Edit Mode. Just place the BP command between the two parts.

Text will not resume at the left margin after previously using the Indent command
You have forgotten to use Cancel Indent in the position you require the text to resume at the left margin.

Headings, which are centred, are underlined from the left margin
You have omitted the Pad Character between the Centre and the Underline commands.

Several lines are not centred properly
Did you count the number of lines correctly? Don't forget to include any line spaces between the text lines.

When previewing text in paged sections (having used the EP command), the text scrolls quickly through the document
You have omitted the Enable Message (EM) command. *See* page 32.

The Get File command does not function properly
Did you remember to use quotation marks before and after the name of the document? Did you have the disk containing that file in the drive? *See* page 35.

The Indent command failed to indent the first line of text
Did you enter the command in mid-line, in which case it will not be effected until the next line? *See* page 38.

The line length is too long for the screen in Preview Mode
You can only preview a line up to 80 characters in length. Therefore, if your line length exceeds this, the extra characters will spill onto a separate line. It should be noted that the width of any left margin is added to the line length when calculating the number of characters used. *See* pages 39 and 40.

Your page is not of the required length
The top and bottom spaces default to 6 lines each. You should add these to your required page length or change the top and bottom spaces to zero. *See* page 44.

Difficulty in setting markers
Remember that only two markers may be set at any one time.

You encounter difficulty with Search and Replace
Did you enter the search string *exactly* as it appears in the text? Was your cursor at the beginning of the document? *See* page 63.

X *You find that you are unable to preview text in 80 column mode*
Has the characters free value fallen below 15500? If so save a part of your document by using Option 3 to save marked text. This marked section can then be deleted from the computer's memory. Your remaining work should be treated as a separate file. *See* page 68. WORDWISE PLUS users should note that any text in the segments will occupy memory.

When saving a document to disk, the message 'Can't extend' or 'Disk full' appears on the screen
The current disk is full.

The printer fails to operate
Printers need to be on-line to the computer. Locate the necessary switch and check that it is in the correct position. (On the Canon AP400, the switch is located at the back of the machine.)

Two-column print out fails to function
Did you change 'DOCUMENT' in line 15 of the DUALCOL program to the name that you gave to your spooled file?

No space between words that have an embedded command between them

Although there appears to be a space on the screen, this is in fact taken up by the *f2* command. Just insert an extra space.

Index

112

Computer Handbooks

Languages

Assembly Language for the 8086 and 8088   Robert
   Erskine
C Language   Friedman Wagner-Dobler

Business Applications

dBASE III   Peter Gosling
VisiCalc   Peter Gosling
SuperCalc and SuperCalc2   Peter Gosling

Microcomputers

The Amstrad 464 and 664   Boris Allan
The Apricot   Peter Gosling
The Sinclair QL   Guy Langdon and
   David Heckingbottom

Operating Systems

Introduction to Operating Systems
   Lawrence Blackburn and Marcus Taylor

Word Processing

Wordwise and Wordwise+   Wendy Chuter

Pocket Guides

Programming

Programming   John Shelley
BASIC   Roger Hunt
COBOL   Ray Welland
FORTH   Steven Vickers
FORTRAN   Philip Ridler
FORTRAN 77   Clive Page
LOGO   Boris Allan
Pascal   David Watt

Assembly Languages

Assembly Language for the 6502   Bob Bright
Assembly Language for the 8085   Noel Morris
Assembly Language for the MC 68000 Series
   Robert Erskine
Assembly Language for the Z80   Julian Ullmann

Microcomputers

Acorn Electron   Neil Cryer and Pat Cryer
Commodore 64   Boris Allan
Programming for the Apple   John Gray
Programming for the BBC Micro   Neil Cryer
   and Pat Cryer
Sinclair Spectrum   Steven Vickers
The IBM PC   Peter Gosling

Operating Systems

CP/M Lawrence Blackburn and Marcus Taylor
MS-DOS Val King and Dick Waller
PC-DOS Val King and Dick Waller
UNIX Lawrence Blackburn and Marcus Taylor

Word Processors

Introduction to Word Processing Maddie Labinger
IBM Displaywriter Jacquelyne A. Morison
Philips P5020 Peter Flewitt
Wang System 5 Maddie Labinger
WordStar Maddie Labinger